Anonymous

Revenue Law Passed by the General Assembly of the State

of North Carolina at the Session of 1862-1863

Anonymous

Revenue Law Passed by the General Assembly of the State of North Carolina at the Session of 1862-1863

ISBN/EAN: 9783337812133

Printed in Europe, USA, Canada, Australia, Japan

Cover: Foto ©Suzi / pixelio.de

More available books at **www.hansebooks.com**

REVENUE LAW,

PASSED BY THE

GENERAL ASSEMBLY

OF THE

STATE OF NORTH-CAROLINA,

AT THE

SESSION OF 1862-'63.

RALEIGH

W. W. HOLDEN, PRINTER TO THE STATE

1863

REVENUE LAW----1862--'63.

AN ACT ENTITLED "REVENUE."

SECTION 1. *Be it enacted by the General Assembly of the State of North Carolina, and it is hereby enacted by the authority of the same,* That an *ad-valorem* tax of two-fifths of one per cent. be levied for the support of the State Government, the payment of its debts, and the promotion of the general welfare, upon the assessed cash value of the following subjects, to wit : *[Ad-valorem tax of two-fifths of one per cent.]*

(1) Real Estate in this State.

(2.) All slaves in this State (excepting such as the County Courts may have exempted, or may hereafter exempt from taxation on account of bodily or mental infirmity,) to be taxed according to value, which value is to be ascertained by the same persons who assess the value of lands. *[Slaves to be taxed according to value.]*

(3) Money due from solvent debtors, or on hand, or on deposit with individuals, or in the banks, or other corporations, *Provided,* That Confederate and State Treasury Notes shall be considered money, and *Provided further,* that the person listing his money on hand and at interest, shall be allowed to deduct debts owing by him as principal, and also as surety, where the principal is insolvent. *[Money due or on hand.]*

(4) Money invested in manufacturing and steamboat corporations or companies, according to the shares as fixed by the charter ; if the shares be in a corporation, and if there be no incorporation then upon the amount invested ; also money invested in county bonds, or State bonds, issued since the 23d of February, 1861 ; also money invested in every species of trade and traffic, not otherwise taxed herein. *[Money invested in corporations, &c]*

(5) Household and kitchen furniture, owned by any individual above the value of two hundred dollars, excepting articles of furniture hereinafter specifically taxed. *[Household and kitchen furniture.]*

Live stock for sale.

(6) **Horses**, mules, cattle, hogs, and other live stock raised or kept for sale, and not for use by the owner, subject to the further exceptions and exemptions hereinafter
set forth.

Cotton and tobacco on speculation.

(7) All cotton and tobacco, except that which is owned by
the producer, or has been purchased by the owner for his
own use, or that of his family or dependents ; and further,
except such cotton as may have been purchased by any
person or corporation for the purpose of manufacturing,
Provided, that no more cotton held by a manufacturer,
shall be exempt from this tax, than is needed for the con-
sumption of one year.

Exemption.

SEC. 2. The following property shall be exempt from taxation, to wit : All lands or other property belonging to the
Confederate States, or this State, or to any County in this
State, or to the University, colleges, or other institutions of
learning ; all town halls, market houses and other public
structures, and edifices, parsonages, and all lots or squares
kept open for health, use or ornament, belonging to any
city, town or village; all churches and chapels set apart and
appropriated to the exercises of Divine worship, or to the
propagation of the Gospel; and such land or other property
as may be set apart and kept for agricultural societies,
grave-yards belonging to churches, and all other public
structures and other property set apart and used for the
support and comfort of the poor and afflicted; mechanical and farming tools, books, wearing apparel, and arms
for muster, and boats, canoes, notes or sums of the value of
one hundred dollars or less.

Property not taxed two-tenths of 1 per cent. to be list-ed separately.

SEC. 3. The property hereinafter taxed at a higher rate
than two-fifths of one per cent, shall not be liable to the tax
of two-fifths of one per cent., but shall be listed separate
therefrom.

Dividends and profits.

SEC. 4. Every dollar of nett dividend or profit not previously listed, declared, received or due, on or before the first
day of April in each year, upon money or capital invested
in shares in the Bank of Washington, the Merchants Bank
of Newbern, the Bank of Wadesboro', the Bank of Fayetteville, the Commercial Bank of Wilmington, the Farmers'
Bank of North Carolina, the Bank of Charlotte, and the

Bank of Yanceyville, shall pay an annual tax of eight cents, but the same shall not be subject to any county tax.

SEC. 5. The stock or interest held by individuals in all corporations or business shall be listed among the individual property of the holders in the counties where they respectively reside.

Stock, &c., to be listed in the counties where the owners reside.

SEC. 6. The taxes shall be annually collected, and paid as follows: First, to the sheriffs, on all property and subjects of taxation required to be listed as per schedule A.— Secondly, to the sheriffs on all property and subjects of taxation, which are not required to be listed, but an account of which is to be rendered upon oath to the sheriffs and to the Treasurer of the State as per exhibit C.

When collected, and to whom paid.

SEC. 7. At the first Court of Pleas and Quarter Sessions for each county, held on or before the first Monday in March, and at the same term every two years thereafter, the court shall appoint one justice of the peace and two free-holders, men of skill and probity, for each Captain's district, or for each school district, at the option of the court, who shall be styled the district board of valuation of their respective districts; the clerk shall issue a notice of his appointment to each man within five days after adjournment of the court. If the court shall fail to make the required appointments, or should from any cause a vacancy occur, any three justices of the peace may make the required appointments or fill the vacancy.

District board of valuation, and when appointed.

SEC. 8. This district board of valuation shall, as near as practicable, ascertain the cash value of every tract of land, or other real estate with the improvements thereon, situate in their district, and also the cash value of every slave required to be listed for taxation in their district, either by viewing the same or otherwise.

Board to ascertain cash value.

SEC. 9. In estimating the value, the board may call and swear witnesses to testify thereto, and they shall take into the estimate any fishery appurtenant thereto, or used with the land; also, all mines of metal, stone or coal, or other material discovered or supposed to exist, whereby the price of land is enhanced; also all machinery and fixtures for manufacturing or mechanical purposes, that have been erected or used on the land. When a tract of land shall be

May call and swear witnesses.

in one or more districts, the board of the district in which
the owner resides shall ascertain the value of whole tract,
and if the owner resides in neither of the districts, the board
of the district in which the larger part may be, shall ascertain the value of the whole.

Owner or agent to furnish list.

SEC. 10. The owner of the land or slaves, or if he be a
non-resident, his agent shall furnish the district board with
a list, including land entries, setting forth the separate tracts,
and also the several contiguous bodies or tracts of land
owned by him in the district, together with the names of
the water courses, or other noted places on or nearest to
which they may be situated, and the number of acres in
each separate tract or contiguous body of land, and also the
names, ages and number of slaves he may be bound to list.

Town lots.

SEC. 11. Town lots shall be listed separately, and each lot
be numbered according to the plot of the town; each separate body or tract of land, and each town lot shall be
separately and distinctly valued and returned.

Oath.

SEC. 12. The district boards shall, in each case, administer
the following oath to the persons furnishing the required
list: You, A. B., do solemnly swear, that the list by you
furnished, contains a full and fair statement of every tract
of land and town lot and slaves in this district, for the taxes
of which you are liable, either in your own right or the
right of any other person, either as guardian, attorney, agent
or trustee, or in any other manner whatsoever, to the best
of your knowledge and belief, so help you God.

Refusal to make oath.

SEC. 13. If any person shall refuse to furnish the list
required above, or to take the oath prescribed in the preceding section, he shall be guilty of a misdemeanor, and
the justices of the peace of said board shall bind him over
to appear at the next term of the Superior Court of the
county to answer the charge, and on conviction or submission, he shall be fined at the discretion of the Court.

Non-residents.

SEC. 14. When the owner of the land and slave or slaves,
or if he be a non-resident of the State, his agent be not a
resident of the district where the land is situated and the
slaves required to be listed, the required list with affidavits
of the same import as the above required oath subscribed
and sworn to before and certified by a justice of the peace,

may be transmitted to the district board of valuation, and if received, before the board shall be ready to value the land and slaves contained in the list, such list shall be received as though tendered and sworn to by the owner or agent in person.

SEC. 15. When the board of valuation are not furnished with a list sworn to as above required, or the owner or agent refuses to answer to the correctness of the statements as to the number of acres contained in any tract of land, they may procure a county or other surveyor and have the same surveyed; and the surveyor may recover the amount of his fees and all expenses out of the owner of the land, before a justice of the peace by warrant or attachment, and the board may examine witnesses on oath as to the number and description of the slaves. *When list is not furnished.*

SEC. 16. The district boards of valuation shall, as soon as practicable, after their appointment, proceed to value all real property and slaves required to be listed in their respective districts as above directed, complete the list by the first Monday of April after their appointment, and annex the following affidavit subscribed and sworn to before a justice of the peace, who shall certify the same: We do solemnly swear that we have diligently enquired and do not believe that there is any real property or slaves required to be listed in the —— district of —— county subject to taxation, that is not entered and valued in the above list; and the foregoing valuation is in our judgment and belief the actual value thereof in cash, and that in assessing the same, we have endeavored to do equal justice to the public and to the individuals concerned, so help us God. This list and valuation shall remain in the hands of the justice of the peace of the board, and be open to the inspection of any one who wishes to examine it until returned as hereinafter directed. *Boards to complete valuation by first Monday of April.* *Affidavit.*

SEC. 17. On the Thursday subsequent to the first Monday of April, after the appointment of the district boards of valuation, the persons who were appointed as justices of the peace to be members of the different district boards, shall meet at the court-house and organize themselves into a county board of valuation by electing by ballot one of their *Justices to meet.*

members chairman and another secretary. In case a justice of the peace of any district board, from any cause, cannot attend, the elder of the two members of the board shall take his place.

Boards to make return of lists.

SEC. 18. To this county board of valuation shall the district boards of valuation make returns of their lists. The board shall carefully examine and compare all the lists, and if, in their opinion, the real property and slaves throughout the county shall not have been assessed by a uniform standard of value, they may re-assess any district, or any separate tract or tracts or lots of land, and also any slave or slaves.

When valued too high.

SEC. 19. If any one deem that too high a valuation was put on his land or slave or slaves, he may apply to the county board of valuation for redress, and they shall duly consider the case, and decide as in their judgment is right; the board may call, swear and examine witnesses, or in person view the land or slaves about the value of which they are in doubt.

Quorum.

SEC. 20. Two thirds of the entire number of the members composing the county board of valuation shall form a quorum for the transaction of business, and the decision of a majority of the members present shall stand as the decision of the board.

When valued too low.

SEC. 21. If in the opinion of the county board of valuation, any tract or tracts of land, or town lots, or slave or slaves have been assessed at too low a value, they shall make lists of such tracts, or lots and slaves, and post them on at least two conspicuous places in the court house, at the time of their adjournment. After they shall have examined and compared the lists, heard the complaints of all who may feel themselves aggrieved by the valuation of their property, the board shall post the lists as above required, and adjourn until the fourth Monday of April, when they shall again meet at the court house, hear the complaints of all who may feel themselves aggrieved by their former action, as by the original valuation, and decide each case as to them may appear right; and from this decision there shall be no appeal.

SEC. 22. When the county boards of valuation shall have

performed the duty on them imposed, they shall return the lists received of the district boards of valuations, as by them revised and corrected, to the clerk of the county court, before whom they shall subscribe and swear to the following affidavit annexed to the list returned: " We solemnly swear that the foregoing lists have been carefully examined and compared, and in our judgment and belief they do, as now corrected, exhibit the actual cash value of every tract or lot of land in this county, with the improvements thereon and privileges thereto attached, and of the slaves required to be listed in this county ; and in the discharge of our duties, we have endeavored to do equal justice to the public and the individuals concerned, so help us God."

SEC. 23. Each member of the county and district boards of valuation shall receive out of the county treasury such compensation as the County Court may allow, not exceeding three dollars per day, for the time he may have been engaged in the discharge of his duties.

SEC. 24. At the first Court of Pleas and Quarter Sessions of each county, which shall be held on or after the first day of January in each and every year, except in cases wherein a special Court is hereinafter provided for, the Court shall appoint for each captain's district or for each school district, at the option of the Court, a justice of the peace or a freeeolder of known skill and probity, to take the lists of taxable subjects, and the names of such takers of the tax lists, with their respective districts, shall, during the term, be advertised at the court house by the clerk.

SEC. 25. If the Court shall fail from any cause to make such appointment, any three justices of the peace of the county may meet at the office of the clerk of the County Court, on or after the first Monday of April, and appoint the takers of the tax lists for the county, or supply any vacancy arising from death or incapacity to act, and the clerk shall record the same.

SEC. 26. The clerk shall issue notice of all appointments of takers of tax lists as soon as made to the sheriff, who shall serve them within ten days upon the appointees, whose duty it shall be to advertise at their several places

in their respective districts at least ten days before the time
of listing the places and times, when and where he will
attend for the purpose of receiving the list of taxables,
which lists he shall take during the last twenty working days
in April; they shall perfect their lists and return them to
the clerk of the county court on or before the second day
of May.

Refusal or failure.

SEC. 27. If any person appointed to take the lists of taxables shall refuse, or willfully fail to discharge the duties of
his appointment, he shall be deemed guilty of a misdemeanor.

Oath.

SEC. 28. Every person appointed to take the lists of taxables before he enters upon the duties of his appointment,
shall take the following oath, to be administered by any
justice of the peace, to-wit: I, (A. B.,) do solemnly swear
that I will perform all my duties as taker of the tax lists for
the district for which I have been appointed, according to
my best knowledge and ability, so help me God.

**Owner to fur-
nish written
list of taxables.**

SEC. 29. It shall be the duty of every one liable to pay
tax, residing in any district, or having property therein
liable to taxation, at the time and place appointed by the
taker of the lists, to furnish him a written list of his taxables, mentioned in section first of this bill and in schedule
A, hereafter set forth, setting forth the number of acres of
land he is bound to list, on what waters situate, the valuation of each tract of land, and the number, ages and value
of his slaves, as assessed by the board of assessors next
preceding the time of listing, and any other slaves subse-
quently acquired, and his estimate of value of such articles,
or subjects of taxation not mentioned in the first section of
this act, as are taxed *ad-valorem;* and such listing and valuation shall have reference to the property owned and the
subjects of taxation held by the tax-payer and its value on
the first day of April next before the listing thereof, and
the taker of the tax list shall administer to the person fur-

Oath.

nishing said list the following oath: You solemnly swear
that the list by you furnished contains a full statement of
all the property and subjects of taxation which you are
bound to list either in your own right or in right of any
other person, and that the property valued by you is not

worth more in cash than the valuation annexed, to the best of your knowledge and belief; *Provided, however*, that in the year 1863 the taker of the tax lists shall not take the lists of lands and slaves, but they shall be ascertained by the clerk of the county court, and entered by him on the tax list to be furnished to the sheriff or tax collector, from the lists of the assessors, and after the year 1863 and until another assessment of slaves, they shall be listed at the same valuation, *Provided, however*, that when the tax lister shall make oath in writing that any slave has become greatly impaired in value by reason of disease, or other bodily or mental infirmity, he may list such slave at such price as he may state on oath is the then present value of such slave, and where a slave shall have been acquired after the assessment, the person listing shall list him at the same value at which he was listed by his former owner if known to him, and if not known to him, he shall file a written affidavit stating his cash value on the first day of April preceding such listing, and as to the slaves born after the assessment, the lister shall be required to state on oath their cash value on the first day of April preceding, and they shall be listed accordingly. *(Special provision for 1863.)*

SEC. 30. Every taker of the tax lists shall be allowed such compensation for his services as the county court may, in its discretion allow, to be paid out of the county treasury. *(Compensation.)*

SEC. 31. Every taker of the tax list after the year 1863, shall be furnished by the clerk of the county court, with a fair copy of the return made by the last board of valuation of the real estate and slaves in his district, and with the necessary printed form of tax bill to be furnished by the Comptroller, under the provisions of this act. *(Takers of tax lists to be furnished lists by the clerk.)*

SEC. 32. The comptroller at the public cost, shall have prepared and printed, as they may be needed, forms of tax lists, with all the articles and subjects of taxation to be listed by virtue of this act, mentioned separately over the heads of parallel columns, in which the amount or quantity, or description of each article or subject to be listed, is to be set down; and he shall annually furnish to each county court clerk, for the use of the county revenue officers, such other blanks as he may deem necessary. *(The Comptroller to have tax lists prepared.)*

How takers shall proceed.

SEC. 33. The taker of the tax list shall set down each article or subject in its proper column against the name of the person listing, arranged in alphabetical order, and return the same to the clerk of the county court as required in section 8.

Oath.

SEC. 34. In the return of said lists the tax listor shall annex the following affidavit: "I solemnly swear that 1 have diligently inquired, and have no just reason to believe that there is any property or other subjects of taxation in my district, not entered and valued, (where the same is required to be valued by the owner) in the above list, with the following exceptions, (here enumerating the exceptions) so help me God."

The clerk to deliver the tax lists to the sheriff by the 25th of June.

SEC. 35. The clerk of the county court annually, on or before the twenty-fifth of June shall deliver to the sheriff of the county a fair and accurate copy of the tax lists, (inserting therein) for the year 1863, the land and slaves, from the list returned to him by the assessors, in alphabetical order, which contain the public tax, or tax payable to the public treasurer, and the taxes payable to the county court. It shall set forth the separate amount due from each subject of taxation, and extend the aggregate amount due from each person in columns ; and if any clerk shall fail to furnish the sheriff at the time prescribed with such copy, he shall be deemed guilty of a misdemeanor, and the sheriff shall inform the grand jury thereof.

The clerks to make record.

Sec. 36. The clerks shall record the returns at length, made by the takers of the tax lists in alphabetical order, keeping the return of each district separate from the others.

Clerk to return an abstract to the Comptroller.

SEC. 37. The clerk on or before the first day of August in each year, shall return to the comptroller an abstract of the same, showing the number of acres of land, and their value, and the value of town lots, and the number of white and free black polls, the number and value of the slaves separately, and specify every other subject of taxation, and the amount of State tax due on each subject, and the amount of the whole; at the same time the clerk shall return to the comptroller an abstract of the poor, county and school taxes, paid in his county, setting forth separately the tax levied on each poll, and on each other subject of taxation, and also the gross amount of taxes imposed for county purposes.

SEC. 38. If any clerk shall fail to perform the duties pre- *Forfeiture of the clerks, &c.* scribed by the preceding section, or shall fail to return to the comptroller a copy of the sheriff's returns made, sworn to and subscribed as required in section —— of this act, he shall forfeit and pay to the State one thousand dollars, to be recovered against him and the sureties of his official bond in the superior court of Wake county at the term next after the default, on motion of the Attorney General, and it shall be the duty of the comptroller to inform the Attorney General of such default.

SEC. 39. For services of clerks in relation to taxes where *Compensation.* no fees are specially provided for in this act, they shall be paid by the county courts such sums as said courts may deem reasonable and just.

SEC. 40. The sheriff shall forthwith proceed to collect said *Deputy sheriff to be sworn.* taxes, and when he shall collect by his deputies, who are not sworn as others, such persons shall, in open court, or before a justice of the peace of the county, take an oath faithfully and honestly to account for the same, with the sheriff or other person authorized to receive them.

SEC. 41. The sheriff shall give to each tax-payer one receipt *Receipts.* for the amount of his taxes, specifying how much is for State taxes and how much for county taxes.

SEC. 42. If any sheriff shall die during the time appointed *On the death of a sheriff.* for collecting taxes, his sureties may collect them, and for that purpose shall have all the powers of collecting the same of the collectors and tax-payers, which the sheriff would have had, and shall be subject to all the remedies for collection and settlement of the taxes on their bond or otherwise, as might have been had against the sheriff if he had lived.

SEC. 43. The sheriff and (in case of his death) his sureties *Time for settlement.* shall have one year and no longer from the day prescribed for his settlement and payment of the State taxes, to finish the collection of all taxes; but this extension of time shall not extend the time of the settlement of the taxes.

SEC. 44. The sheriff shall collect the taxes as they are set down in the list, and moreover, shall collect of all persons

Sheriff to collect according to the lists, &c.
whose taxables are not listed, double the taxes imposed on the same subjects; and as to any land not listed, which may not have been assessed at the last assessment, the same in estimating the double tax, shall be deemed to be of the value by the acre, of the highest valued tract adjoining thereto; and as to any personal property not listed, herein taxed according to value, the sheriff may call on a justice of the peace of the vicinage, who shall value the same and put his valuation in writing, and the sheriff shall collect a double tax on such valuation.

Sheriff to advertise.
SEC. 45. Immediately on receiving the tax list, the sheriff shall advertise the fact, and that he holds them ready for inspection. He shall also request therein, all persons to inform him of any taxables which are not listed; for the more efficient collection of the taxes, the sheriff at any time, from the delivery to him of the lists, till the first day of October, in the next year may, and if there be need, shall distrain and sell the property of the tax payer to satisfy the same, selling first his personal and then his real estate.

Compensation.
SEC. 46. In each case in which the sheriff collects by distress, he shall be entitled to an extra compensation of forty cents, to be collected with the tax.

Persons about to remove.
SEC. 47. If any person liable for taxes on other subjects than land, shall [be] about to remove from the county, after listing time, and before the period for collection, the sheriff shall make affidavit thereof before the clerk, and obtain from him a certificate of the amount of such person's tax, and forthwith collect the same.

Court to issue a fi. fa. in certain cases.
SEC. 48. If any person be liable for taxes in any county wherein he shall have no property, but shall be supposed to have property in some other county, and will not pay his tax, the sheriff shall report the fact to the county court held next after the first day of October, and thereupon the court shall direct the clerk to issue a *fieri facias* to the sheriff of that county, returnable to the court whence it issues for such tax, and the cost of process and executing the same, which the sheriff shall execute in the manner of writs of execution in other cases, and the tax collected thereon, shall be paid to the clerk of the court, and by him paid to the sheriff to be accounted for as other taxes.

Sec. 49. The sale under distress of personal estate for taxes shall be advertised ten days previous thereto, at three public places in the district wherein the delinquent tax payer shall reside, and if he reside not in the county then in the district where the taxables were or ought to have been listed; and the amount of tax shall be stated in the advertisement.

Sales to be advertised.

Sec. 50. The sale of land for taxes due thereon, shall be made under the following rules:

Rules for advertising sales for taxes

(1) The sheriff shall return to the court of pleas and quarter sessions of his county, held next after the first day of January, a list of the tracts of land which he proposes to sell for taxes, therein mentioning the owner or the supposed owner of each tract, and if such owner be unknown, the last known or reputed owner, the situation of the tracts and the amount of taxes for which they are respectively to be sold, which list shall be read aloud in open court, recorded by the clerk upon the minutes of the court, and a copy thereof shall be put up in some public part of the court house.

Sheriff to make returns to the county court

(2) The county court shall order the clerk of the court to issue notice to every person whose land is returned as aforesaid; and a copy of the notice shall be served by the sheriff on the owner or agent and returned to the next county court; and if the owner be a non-resident, the clerk shall publish the same in some newspaper printed in the State, in which advertisement shall be mentioned the situation of the land, the streams on or near which it lies, the estimated quantity, the names of the owners, where they are known, and the names of the tenants of the same.

The court to order clerk to notify, &c

(3) The sales shall be made within the two terms next succeeding the term when the returns are made of lands to be sold, and at such place in the county as is directed for the sale of land under execution; and the whole expense attendant on the advertising and sale shall be chargeable on the lands and raised at the sale.

When returns are to be made

(4.) The whole tract or contiguous body of land belonging to one delinquent person or company, shall be set up for sale at the same time, and the bid shall be struck off to him who will pay the amount of taxes, with the expenses aforesaid, for the smallest part of the land.

The sheriff to
return a list of
tracts sold.
(5.) At the second term next succeeding the term when the returns are made of lands to be sold, the sheriff shall return a list of the tracts actually sold for taxes, the quantity of the tract bought and to be laid off, the name of the purchasers and the sum paid to the sheriff for taxes and charges, which list shall be read aloud by the clerk in open court, shall be recorded in the minutes of the court, and a copy thereof shall be put up by the clerk during the term in some public part of the court house.

Failure of
sheriff.
Sec. 51. If any sheriff or clerk shall fail to perform any of the duties prescribed in sections 47 and 48 of this act, he shall forfeit and pay to the person aggrieved one hundred dollars, and he and his sureties shall moreover be liable for all such damages as any person may sustain by reason of such default.

The lands of
infants, &c.,
not to be sold.
Sec. 52. The land of an infant, lunatic, or person *non compos mentis,* shall not be sold for taxes, *Provided, however,* that when land may be owned by such persons in common with another or others, free of such disability, the share or interest of the person so free, shall be subject to be sold for the taxes due on the whole tract; but before setting apart the quantity bid off, the purchaser, by petition, shall cause the tract to be divided among the tenants in common, and the share or interest of the defaulting tax-payer being set apart, the purchaser may proceed to lay off on such share the quantity by him bid off and secure the title as before provided; and the time necessarily employed in procuring such division shall not be reckoned against the purchasers.

Owner may
redeem.
Sec. 53. The owner of land sold for taxes under section 50 of this act, his heirs, executors or administrators or any other person for them, may redeem the same from the purchaser, at any time within one year after the sale, by paying or tendering in payment to the purchaser or to the county court clerk of the county where the land lies, the full amount paid to the sheriff and twenty-five per cent thereon.

If not re-
deemed, what
to be done.
Sec. 54. If the land so sold, shall not be redeemed within the period aforesaid, the purchaser may, at the end of that time, select the quantity of land struck off to him out of

any part of the tract or body; of which the same was bid off, the said quantity to be laid off in one compact body as nearly square as may be, and adjoining to some of the outlines of the whole tract or body of land.

SEC. 55. Within one year after the time of redemption shall have passed, the purchaser, at his own cost, his heirs, executors or administrators, or any of them, may procure the quantity bid off to be surveyed by the county surveyor, who shall make out and certify, under his hand, a fair plot of the survey, with the courses and distances fairly and truly set forth, and if the county surveyor, on request, shall fail to make such survey and plot, then any other surveyor may make and certify the same.

The purchaser may have land surveyed a year after the time of redemption.

SEC. 56. The sheriff on being presented with such certified plot, within the year after the time of redemption is passed, shall convey to the purchaser the land therein contained.

The sheriff to make a title, if sold by him.

SEC. 57. When by any provision of the law, any sheriff or officer other than the person who sold for the taxes, shall be authorized to execute a conveyance for the land, the purchaser shall apply to the county court, and on showing to the court that such purchase has been made, and the price paid to the sheriff who sold, and that he has paid the other taxes since accruing thereon, the court shall direct the present sheriff to execute a deed on the purchaser's producing to him a certified plot and survey as is provided for in sections 55 and 56 of this act.

Title in other cases.

SEC. 58. The purchaser of land, sold for taxes, under section 50 of this act, shall be considered as taking and holding the same subject to all the taxes accrued from the first day of April in the year preceding the purchase.

Purchasers under Sec. 50.

SEC. 59. If any county surveyor, being required within two months after the survey may be lawfully made, to survey the land bid off at sale for taxes, shall wilfully fail to do so within four months after such request, he shall forfeit and pay to the purchaser, or his executor or administrator, one hundred dollars.

Forfeit of county surveyor.

SEC. 60. If no person will bid a less quantity than the whole land, for the taxes, the bid shall be deemed the bid of the State, and the land shall be struck off to the State as the purchaser, and the sheriff shall report in writing to the

When to be deemed the bid of the State

county court at the time he returns the list of lands sold for taxes, what and whose lands are thus struck off to the State, describing them particularly, which report shall be recorded on the minutes of the court, and thereupon the title of said lands shall be deemed to have been vested in the State from the time of purchase.

The clerk to make and certify two copies. SEC. 61. The clerk shall, within twenty days after the return of the sheriff's report of the land sold to the State, make and certify two copies thereof, one of which he shall transmit to the comptroller and the other deliver to the sheriff, (or his sureties when they act) who shall deposit the same with the Secretary of State, to be by him recorded, and the secretary shall grant to the sheriff a certificate, setting forth what and whose land and the quantity and value thereof, have been sold for the taxes and struck off to the State.

Penalty for not making return. SEC. 62. If any sheriff or other person authorized thereto, shall sell for taxes and strike off any land to the State, and shall fail duly to report the same to the county court, or to duly obtain and deposit a copy thereof with the Secretary of State, the comptroller shall, in his report to the treasurer, charge such sheriff (or other person acting in his stead) with the sum of two thousand dollars, and the treasurer shall recover the same as an unpaid tax.

How redeemed. SEC. 63. Lands bid off for the State may be redeemed in like time, and under the same rules and regulations as those purchased by individuals, except the payment (which shall be double in amount of all taxes for which they were sold) shall be made to the treasurer, and on his certificate thereof the Secretary of State shall, on being paid his fees issue a grant to the original proprietor, his heirs or assigns, and at the same time shall certify the payment to the comptroller.

Liable to entry. SEC. 64. Lands bid off for the State, shall, as to the person for whose tax the same is sold, his heirs or assigns, be liable to be entered as vacant lands, subject, nevertheless, to the right of redemption within the time prescribed.

Sureties may report. SEC. 65. When land shall be sold for its tax, and the sheriff shall die, or otherwise become unable to report his sales, his sureties may report the same within the time prescribed, and shall proceed as to the land bid off by the State, in the same manner as the sheriff might.

SEC. 66. When any person shall sell his real property, *Real estate bound.* and shall have no estate within reach of the sheriff, to satisfy the taxes due from him on any subject of taxation, the real property shall be bound for all such taxes.

SEC. 67. Every conveyance made by any deceased person, *Conveyance to avoid taxes void.* with the fraudulent intent to evade the collection of any taxes by this act imposed, shall as against the State be void, and the taxes shall be chargeable at the suit of the State of North Carolina, on the property conveyed in the hands of vendees, donors and assignees.

SEC. 68. If the sheriff, or other person shall discover that *Lands not assessed.* any land has not been assessed, he shall make it known to the county court, whereupon a board shall be appointed to assess the same, who shall proceed in the manner herein provided, and the court shall ascertain the amount of tax which, within the ten preceding years, the land has been liable for but not paid, and the sheriff shall be ordered forthwith to collect treble the amount with interest, of all such tax, by distress or otherwise.

SEC. 69. It shall be the duty of the sheriff to inform the *Sheriffs to inform Attorney General &c.* attorney general, and the solicitors of the State, for the circuits and counties. concerning all omissions by tax payers, done in their respective counties to defraud the State of its revenue ; and the attorney general and solicitors for the State for circuits, upon information or good cause of suspicion, that any person has wilfully omitted to return his tax list, or has wilfully failed to file an accurate and fair list of all the property, estate and subjects on and for which he is liable to be taxed, shall file a bill in equity against the person so in default, and the answer of the defendant shall not be competent against him in any criminal or penal prosecution; and whenever a suit is brought, or a bill filed in behalf of the State, under any provisions of this act, it shall be done in the name of the State of North Carolina.

2

SCHEDULE A.

Subjects to be listed.   SEC. 70. The following subjects shall be annually listed in addition to those mentioned in the first section of this act, and taken as herein specified :

Polls.   (1) Every taxable poll, one dollar and twenty cents; *Provided* that the county court may exempt such poor and infirm persons as they may declare and record fit subjects of exemption ; and, *Provided further*, that soldiers in the actual service of the Confederate or State government, shall not be required to list or pay a full tax.

Toll Gates.   (2) Every toll gate on a turnpike road, and every toll bridge, and every ferry 2½ per cent on amount of receipts during the year, and all keepers of houses of public entertainment, whether in town or country, whose annual receipts amount to three hundred dollars or more, a tax of one per cent on the receipts.

Gates across highways.   (3) Every gate, permitted by the county court to be erected across a highway, fifteen dollars.

Note shavers.   (4) Every note shaver, or person who buys any note or notes, bond or bonds made by individuals shall list the profits made and received, or secured on all such purchases made by him during the year ending on the first day of July, whether made for cash or in exchange for other notes or bonds, and pay a tax of ten per cent on the aggregate amount of such profits, in addition to the tax imposed by this act on the interest he may receive on such notes or bonds ; *Provided*, that there shall be no deduction made from the profits in consequence of any losses sustained.

Negro traders.   (5) Every person resident in this State, engaged in the business of buying and selling slaves, whether the purchases be made in or out of the State for cash or on a credit, one-half of one per cent on the total amount of all his purchases, during the twelve months preceding the first day of April.

Persons buying slaves to sell again.   (6) Every person resident in this State, not a regular trader in slaves, who may buy a slave or slaves to sell again, whether such purchase be made in or out of the State, for cash or on credit, one-half of one per cent on the total amount of his purchases during the twelve months ending the 31st of March of each year.

(7.) Every carriage, buggy or other vehicle kept for pleasure or the conveyance of persons, of the value of fifty dollars or upwards, one per cent on its value. Every stud horse or jackass let to mares for a price, belonging to a resident of the State, six dollars, unless the highest price demanded for the season for one mare shall exceed that sum, in which case the amount thus demanded shall be paid as a tax, such jack or stud to be listed, and the tax paid in the county in which the owner resides. *Vehicles.*

(8.) All gold and silver plate, gold and silver-plated ware and jewelry worn by males, including watch chains, seals and keys, where collectively of greater value than twenty-five dollars, one per cent on their entire value. *Gold and silver plate, jewelry, &c.*

(9.) Every watch except those kept for sale, one per cent on their value; every harp in use $2.50; every piano in use $1.50; every gold headed cane in use $1.00; every silver headed cane in use 50 cents. *Watches, &c.*

(10.) Every resident surgeon, dentist, physician, lawyer, portrait or miniature painter, daguerrean artist, or other person taking likenessess of the human face, and every commission merchant, factor, produce broker and auctioneer, every State and county officer, every president and cashier, superintendent or treasurer of any bank, railroad, or other incorporated company, whose total annual receipts and income in the way of practice, fees, wages, perquisites and emoluments, amount to or are worth one thousand dollars or upwards, one per cent on such total receipts and income; *Provided* that this clause shall not be construed to apply to the salaries of the judges of the supreme or superior courts of law, nor to the salaries of military officers in the actual field service of the Confederate or State governments, nor to the salary of the Governor. *Surgeons, dentists, &c.*

(11.) Every head of a family shall list all his dogs above two on any one plantation, including those owned by his slaves, or any other person resident on his land or living in his family; and every person not the head of a family shall list all the dogs owned by him self or his slaves except one, and a tax of one dollar shall be collected on each dog listed; *Dogs.*

Provided, however, that no one shall be required to list dogs under eight months old : *Provided, however,* that the county courts of each county, a majority of the justices being present, in their discretion may levy the above taxes on dogs, and the taxes collected, levied under this section shall be for county purposes.

Dead Heads.

(12.) Every person who shall have traveled any railroad in this State in which the State has an interest as a stockholder, or with which the State may have exchanged its bonds, paying nothing, (commonly known by the name of dead-heads) or paying less than two and a half cents per mile, or any member of whose family shall have so traveled, (excepting the officials and employees travelling in the actual discharge of their duties as officials or employees, and excepting also ministers of the gospel travelling in the actual discharge of their religious functions,) shall list the number of miles he or any member of his family shall have so traveled the year preceding the first day of April, and shall pay a tax of two and a half cents per mile for each mile so traveled by him or by any member of his family, and on failure or refusal so to list, he shall be guilty of a misdemeanor, and on conviction, shall pay a fine of not less than one hundred dollars.

Brandy distillers.

(13.) Every person who shall have distilled brandy for himself, for sale, and every one who shall have had brandy distilled for sale, the year preceding the first day of April in every year, shall list the number of gallons so distilled, and pay a tax of ten cents per gallon.

Liquor dealers.

(14.) Every resident of the State, who may have brought into the State, or who may have bought from a non-resident, whether by sample or otherwise, spirituous liquors, wines or cordials, for the purpose of sale, twenty per cent on the amount of his profits, and every person who may have bought to sell again, spirituous liquors, distilled in this State, ten per cent on the amount of his profits.

Dividends and profits.

(15.) On every dollar of nett profit or dividend declared, received or due during the year preceding the first of April in each year, (and not previously listed) upon money or capital invested in manufacturing cotton or woolen goods, leather, or articles made of leather, iron and tobacco, and also on every dollar of nett profit or dividend on money invested in steamboat companies, (whether incorporated or not,) and in railroads a tax of two cents.

(16.) Upon all real and personal estate, whether legal or equitable, above the value of one hundred dollars, situated in this State, which shall descend or be devised or bequeathed to any collateral relation or person, other than a lineal ancestor or descendent, or the husband or wife of the deceased, or husband or wife of such ancestor or descendant, or to which such collateral relation may become entitled under the law for the distribution of intestate estates, and which real and personal estate may not be required in payment of debts and other liabilities, the following *per centum* tax upon the value thereof shall be paid. Collateral descents.

Class 1. If such collateral relation be a brother or sister, a tax of one per cent.

Class 2. If such collateral relation be a brother or a sister of the father or the mother of the deceased, or child of such brother or sister, a tax of two per cent.

Class 3. If such collateral relation be a more remote relation, or the devisee or legatee be a stranger, a tax of three per cent.

(17.) The real estate liable to taxation shall be listed by the devisee or heir in a separate column, designating its proper per cent tax.

(18.) The personal estate shall be liable to the tax in the hands of the executor or administrator, and shall be paid by him before his administration account is audited or the estate settled to the sheriff of the county.

(19.) If the real estate descended or devised shall not be the entire inheritance, the heir or devisee shall pay a *pro rata* tax corresponding with the relative value of his estate or interest.

(20.) If the legacy or distributive share to be received, shall not be the entire property, such legatee or distributes shall, in like manner, pay a *pro rata* part of the tax, according to the value of his interest.

(21.) Whenever the personal property in the hands of such executor or administrator, (the same not being needed to be converted into money in the course of the administration) shall be of uncertain value, he shall apply to the county court, to appoint three impartial men of probity to assess the value thereof, and such assessment being returned to court and confirmed, shall be conclusive of the value.

All property to be listed in possession on 1st of April.

Sec. 71. Every person shall, at such time and place as shall be designated by the persons appointed to take the list of taxables, list all the real and personal estate, and other taxable subjects enumerated in schedule A of this act, which were his property or in his possession, or were the subjects of taxation on the first day of April of that year.

Executors, &c., to list property of testators, &c.

Sec. 72. Lists of taxables of testators, intestates, minors, lunatics, insane persons, absentees, and other estates held in trust, shall be rendered by the executor, administrator, guardian, agent, trustee, or *cesqui que trust*, as the case may be.

Real estate to be listed where situated, except in certain cases.

Sec. 73. Real estate shall be listed in the county where situated, and where a tract of land is divided by a county line, shall be listed in the county where the larger portion shall be situated, except when the owner resides in one of the counties in which a portion of the tract is situated, in which case, if he holds the lands in both counties under one title, he shall list in the county in which he resides ; where the Pedee and Yadkin rivers shall be the dividing line between counties, in that case the land shall be listed in the county where the same shall be situated.

When divided the parts to be valued, &c.

Sec. 74. Where any tract of land or town lot shall have been divided, after valuation by the board of valuation, the taker of the tax list shall return the separate valuation of each part, making the aggregate value of the parts equal to the board valuation of the entire tract or lot.

To facilitate collection of tax on collateral descents.

Sec. 75. To facilitate the collection of tax on collaterals, every executor or administrator, shall return in his inventory, whether the estate goes to the lineal or collateral relations of the deceased, or to a stranger, and if to collaterals, the degree of relationship of said collaterals to the deceased, under a penalty of one hundred dollars, to be recovered in the name and to the use of the State.

When to be listed, and where.

Sec. 76. Every poll that is, or will be of the required age on the first day of July of any year, shall be listed that year ; every owner, if in the State, shall list his slaves in the county in which he resides; and if the owner be a non-resident of the State, or a refugee from his county, the hirer or person who has the slaves in possession, shall list the same and pay the taxes. Slaves hired out beyond the limits of the State, shall be listed by the owners as well as those employed within the State; *Provided* that the provisions of this act shall not apply to owners of slaves who have permanently located said slaves beyond the limits of the State, and hire them from year to year in other States.

SEC. 77. Such slaves and other taxable personal estate, as are employed on the land of the owner, shall be listed in the county in which the land is listed.

Slaves to be listed where the land is.

SEC. 78. Every head of a family, or owner of land or town lot, who, on the first day of April, shall have a taxable free person of color as a member of his family, or in his employment, or living on his land or in his house, shall list such person for taxation, and pay the tax.

Free persons of color.

SEC. 79. Personal property, and other subjects of taxation, unless otherwise directed in section 75 [?] shall be listed in the district where the owner or lister resides; but if the owner reside out of the State, they shall be listed in the district where his agent or the person liable for tax may reside.

Personal property, &c.

SEC. 80. That no taker of a tax list shall take the list of any one without administering the oath prescribed in section 29, on pain of paying one hundred dollars to any one who will sue for it; *Provided*, that females, aged and infirm persons, and persons not resident in the county, or absent from the county during the days of listing taxables, may transmit their list to the taker of the tax list, with the foregoing oath subscribed and sworn to before, and certified by a justice of the peace, which list, if transmitted to the taker of the tax lists, on or before the day appointed for taking the lists, shall be entered by him as though sworn to in his presence.

Takers of lists to require oath.

SEC. 81. That if any person shall refuse to take the oath prescribed in section 29, of this act, he shall be deemed guilty of a misdemeanor, and the taker of the tax list shall forthwith commit him to the common jail, unless he will be recognized with sureties, to appear at the next term of the superior court of the county to answer the charge, and on

Refusal to make oath adjudged a misdemeanor.

conviction or submission, he shall be fined one hundred dollars, at least, more than the amount of his taxes.

Taxables may be listed before lists are returned. SEC. 82. That if any person neglect to list his taxables on the day or days appointed for that purpose, he may list it at any time before the lists are returned to the court, under the same rules and regulations as laid down for listing on appointed days on paying, to the person taking the list, twenty-five cents, as compensation for his extra trouble.

Overcharged taxables. SEC. 83. If any one shall be charged with more polls, or other subjects of taxation than he is liable for, he may apply to the county court for relief, and if the court shall find that he has cause for complaint, it shall direct the clerk to render a true account thereof, and the account thus rendered, certified by the clerk, shall be returned to the comptroller, who shall credit the sheriff with the overcharge in his settlement of that year.

Clerical errors. SEC. 84. If after the tax list shall be placed in the hands of the sheriff, it shall be made to appear to the county court that there is any clerical error therein, whereby any one shall be charged with more or less polls, or other subjects of taxation, or a greater or less valuation than that fixed by the board of assessors, the court shall direct the clerk to enter a true account thereof upon his minutes, which he shall certify to the comptroller, who shall debit or credit the sheriff accordingly, in his settlement of that year.

Applications for relief. SEC. 85. If the application for relief be made to the court, after the sheriff shall have settled the accounts with the comptroller, the court shall carefully examine the case, and if in its opinion, the applicant is entitled to relief, shall direct the clerk to record on the minute docket, the cause of complaint, and the amount which, in the opinion of the court, should be refunded to the applicant. The clerk shall make out a copy of such record, certify the same under the seal of the court, and deliver it to the applicant, who shall pay to the clerk a fee of fifty cents. Such copy shall then be transmitted to the comptroller of the State, who, on finding the proceedings in conformity with the requirements of this section, shall credit the treasurer of the State with the amount specified, and make an endorsement to that effect, on the transcript. The treasurer shall, on presentation of such copy thus endorsed, pay to the holder of the same, the amount to be refunded.

Schedule B.

Subjects Taxed without being Listed.

Sec. 86. The sheriff shall annually collect the taxes as set forth in this schedule, and grant to each party paying the tax, a license to carry on his business, until the first day of July next ensuing, except in cases where the tax is on non-resident traders in slaves, or horse and mule drovers, in which cases no license shall be required. *Sheriffs to give license.*

(1.) Every company of circus-riders, or exhibitors of collections of animals, seventy-five dollars for each county in which they shall perform or exhibit for reward. Every separate exhibition (commonly known as side-shows,) accompanying such performers or exhibitors, which cannot be seen without the payment of a separate charge, fifteen dollars for each county in which they exhibit for reward. *Circus riders.*

(2.) Every company of stage or theatrical players, or persons performing feats of strength or agility, or exhibiting natural or artificial objects, except amateur performers, twenty dollars for each county in which they exhibit for reward. *Stage players.*

(3.) Every company of itinerant singers or performers on musical instruments, or dancers, or itinerant companies, who, otherwise exhibit for the public amusement, ten dollars for each county in which they exhibit for reward. *Itinerant singers.*

(4.) Every insurance company incorporated out of the State, five per cent upon its gross receipts. *Insurance companies.*

(5.) Every agency of a bank incorporated out of the State, five hundred dollars. *Bank agencies.*

(6.) Every money or exchange, bond or note broker, private banker or agent of a foreign broker or banker, ten per cent upon his profits. *Brokers, &c*

(7.) Every express company six hundred dollars. *Express company.*

(8.) Every public billiard table one hundred and twenty-five dollars; every private billiard table twenty-five dollars; every bagatelle and roulette table fifty dollars. *Billiard tables.*

Bowling Alleys.

(9.) Every public bowling alley, whether called a nine-pin or ten pin alley, or by any other name, fifty dollars; every private bowling alley ten dollars.

Livery stable.

(10.) Every livery stable, or places where horses and vehicles are kept for hire, fifty dollars.

Retailers of liquors.

(11.) Every licensed retailer of spirituous liquors, wines or cordials, or retailer of malt liquors, fifty dollars. In addition to this, such retailer shall list the amount of liquors, wines and cordials, as required in schedule A of this act, and pay the tax there imposed.

Non-resident negro buyers.

(12.) Every non-resident of the State, who, in person or by agent, shall purchase any slave or slaves in this State, shall, immediately after such purchase, become liable to pay a tax of one-half of one per cent on the amount of his purchase, and upon his neglect or failure to pay such tax, he shall forfeit and pay the sum of one hundred dollars, which shall be collected by the sheriff, one-half to his own use and the other half to the use of the State. When the purchase was made by an agent, such agent shall be equally liable for the tax and forfeiture with the principal.

Non-resident negro sellers.

(13.) Every non-resident of the State, who, either in person or by agent, brings a slave or slaves into the State and sells, shall pay one-half of one per cent on the amount of each sale effected. If he fail to pay this tax, the purchaser shall be liable for the same, and the sheriff of the county in which the sale was made, or in which the purchaser resides, shall collect, by distress or otherwise, out of the seller, if to be found in his county, and if the seller is not to be found, out of the buyer.

Slave dealers held to be non-residents unless otherwise proven.

(14.) Every buyer or seller of slaves, shall be held to be a non-resident of the State, unless he produce satisfactory evidence to the sheriff that he is a resident.

Playing cards.

(15.) Every person that sells playing cards, fifty cents per pack on all cards sold by him during the year.

Riding Vehicles.

(16.) Every person that for himself, or as agent for another, at his regular place of business, sells riding vehicles, manufactured out of this State, one per cent on his sales.

Auctioneers.

(17.) Every auctioneer, on all goods, wares or merchandize, placed in his hands by a merchant resident in the State, (whether owner or not,) or by a commission mer-

chant, one per cent on gross amount of sales, and if by
itinerant traders or such as are non-residents of the State,
five per cent on gross amount of sales, subject to all the
regulations and exceptions set forth in the tenth chapter
Revised Code, entitled auctions and auctioneers.

(18) Every merchant, merchant-tailor, jeweller, grocer, druggist, apothecary, produce dealer, commission merchant, factor, produce broker, and every other trader, who, as principal or agent for another, carries on the business of buying and selling goods or wares, merchandise of whatsoever name or description, and who is not taxed on his purchases in some other paragraph of this schedule, one-half of one per cent on the total amount of his purchases, whether made in or out of the State, for cash or on credit; *Provided*, that the value of articles, which are received in payment of goods sold at the usual place of business, shall not be estimated in the amount of purchases. *[Every merchant, grocer, &c.]*

(19.) From and after the first day of January, 1863, every person or corporation manufacturing cotton or woolen cloth, or a mixture of both, cotton, yarn, leather, shoes, boots, flour, salt, implements of husbandry, wagons, wagon-harness, and all articles manufactured out of leather, clothing and iron, and every other person, who, as principal or agent for another, carries on the business of manufacturing any of the foregoing articles, all nett profits above seventy-five per cent upon the cost of production. *[Manufacturers of cotton, wool, &c.]*

(20.) Every dealer in ready-made clothing (ready-made garments for males,) one and one half per cent. on total amount of purchases. *[Ready made clothing.]*

(21.) Every person who, for himself or as agent for another, sells patent medicines or nostrums, ten per cent on amount of his sales. *[Patent medicines.]*

(22.) Every horse or mule drover, or person who receives horses or mules to sell for another, one per cent. on the amount of each sale, due as soon as the sale is effected, and upon his neglect or failure to pay such tax in every county in which he sells, he shall forfeit and pay the sum of one hundred dollars, which shall be collected by the sheriff, by distress or otherwise, one-half to his own use and one-half to the use of the State. *[Horse drovers.]*

(23.) Every stud horse or jackass let to mares for a price, belonging to a non-resident of the State, ten dollars, unless the highest price demanded for the season, for one mare, shall exceed that sum, in which case, the amount thus demanded shall be paid for the license. The payment to one sheriff, and the license under his hand, shall protect the subject, in this paragraph taxed, in any county of this State. Every stud horse or jackass shall be considered as belonging to a non-resident, unless the sheriff is furnished with satisfactory evidence that the owner is a resident of this State.

(24.) Every person that peddles goods, wares or merchandize, not the growth or manufacture of this State, or any drugs, medicines, or nostrums, whether such person travel on foot, with a conveyance, or otherwise, shall first have proved to the county court, that he is a citizen of the Confederate States, and is of good moral character, and shall have obtained from the court, (who may, in its discretion make or refuse) an order to the sheriff to grant him pedlar's license, to expire on the first of July next ensuing. And the sheriff, on production of a copy of such order, certified by the clerk of said court, shall grant such license for his county, on receipt of forty dollars tax ; *Provided*, That not more than one person shall peddle under one license, (2.) That any person who temporarily carries on a business as merchant, in any public place, and then removes his goods, shall be deemed a pedlar. (3.) That nothing in this act contained, shall prevent any person from freely selling live stock, vegetables, fruits, oysters, fish, books, charts, maps, printed music or the articles of his own growth or manufacture.

(25.) Every itinerant who deals in, or puts up lightning rods, or who sells spirituous liquors, wines or cordials, in quantities from one quart to one barrel, shall be under the same rules and restrictions, and be liable to the same tax, as pedlars, except that no order from court shall be required to entitle him to a license ; *Provided*, that any person shall be permitted to sell any spirituous liquors, wines or cordials, made from the products of his own farm, without paying the tax in this paragraph imposed.

(26.) Every company of Gypsies, or any strolling company of persons who make a support by pretending to tell fortunes, horse trading, tinkering or begging, one hundred dollars in each county in which they offer to practice any of their crafts, recoverable out of any property belonging to any one of the company. But nothing herein contained shall be so construed as to exempt them from indictment, or any other penalties now imposed by law. *Gypsies.*

(27.) Every freeman that shall arrive at age, after the first day of July, of every year, may pay his poll tax for State purposes, for that year, to the sheriff or his deputy, before the election without listing. *Poll tax paid to sheriffs in certain cases.*

(28.) If any person, bound to list property in his own right, or the right of another, shall fail to list the same or any part thereof, the sheriff shall collect from him, and of his own proper estate, double the tax imposed on the property or subject not listed: *Provided*, that nothing herein contained shall subject to double tax the estate of a soldier in the service. *Penalty for failure to list*

SEC. 87. The county court may release any person from the payment of a double tax, for failing to list his taxables, in cases where it shall appear to the court, by satisfactory evidence, that such failue occurred by reason of sickness of the party at the time when the list was taken, or when it may appear that he rendered a list, and that his name was omitted to be entered, or was omitted in the duplicate prepared by the taker of the tax lists to be returned to the clerk, or for other sufficient cause, to be judged of by the Court. *Co'y Court may release from double tax.*

SEC. 88. On personal property, in the hands of executors and administrators, bequeathed to, or as distributive shares to collateral relations or strangers, as set forth in schedule A, in connection with real estate descended or devised to collateral relations or strangers, the tax shall be paid to the sheriff direct. *Paid to sheriff direct*

SEC. 89. Every person who is intended to be taxed in paragraphs 15, 16, 17, 18, 19, 20 and 23, of schedule B, and shall have been carrying on his business 12 months before the first day of July of any year, shall render to the sheriff a statement of the amount of his purchases of taxable articles (or sales thereof as the said paragraphs may require) during the year ending on the first day of July, and shall sign and swear to an affidavit that his purchases (or sales as may be required) during that period, did not exceed the amount stated, and on his paying the taxes imposed and enumerated in schedule B, shall be entitled to a license to carry on his business until the first of July next ensuing.

License may be issued on giving bond.

Sec. 90. Every person who is intended to be taxed in paragraphs 15, 16, 17, 18, 19, 20 and 23, of schedule B., commencing to do business, or who shall not have been doing business for twelve months before the first of July, shall pay at the end of the year for which his license is issued, the taxes on his purchases or sales, as set forth in said paragraphs ; and to secure the same, he shall, before license is delivered, enter into bond with good sureties, payable to the State of North Carolina, in such sum as the sheriff may deem sufficient, conditioned that he will render a true statement of his purchases or sales, as by this act required for the period embraced in his license, and pay his taxes thereon on the first day of July, when his license shall expire.

Penalty without license.

Sec. 91. Every person who shall carry on any business intended to be taxed as per schedule B, without having previously obtained a license as required, shall in addition to the taxes, forfeit and pay one hundred dollars, to be collected by distress or otherwise, by the sheriff, one-half to his own use, and the other half to the use of the State.

Penalty for refusal to exhibit license.

Sec. 92. Every person intended to be taxed by paragraphs 1, 2, 3, 22, 23, 24 and 25, of schedule B, shall show his license to any justice of the peace or constable who may demand a view thereof, and it shall be the duty of every constable to demand such a view, and if such person fail to exhibit his license on demand thus made, he shall forfeit and pay one hundred dollars, recoverable on a warrant before a justice of the peace, one-half to the person suing out the warrant, and the other half to the use of the State, to be paid over to the sheriff and accounted for as taxes.

Sheriffs to keep a record of taxes collected from clerks.

Sec. 93. Every sheriff shall keep a record of the taxes collected by him from the clerks of courts and under schedule B, of this act, and of all forfeitures, arrears for insolvents, double taxes and taxes on unlisted subjects, and on or before the second Monday in August, shall deliver to the clerk of the county court, a statement setting forth all the sums received to that date, and not previously accounted for, the date of receipt, the person from whom received, the amount received from such person, the subjects on which received, and the aggregate amount, accompanied by an affidavit, signed and sworn to before the clerk and attested by him, that the statement is correct, and that no receipt has been omitted. And the clerk before the third Monday in August, shall send a duplicate of said statement and affidavit to the comptroller of the State, register the same in a book kept in his office for that purpose, and keep a copy of the same posted in a conspicuous place in the court house, until the first day of January next ensuing.

SEC. 94. The clerk, on application of the sheriff, shall deliver to him a true abstract of such return, which the sheriff shall deliver to the comptroller when he settles his accounts; and if any sheriff shall fail to deliver such abstract to the comptroller, the comptroller shall add to the taxes for which such sheriff is liable one thousand dollars, and so report his account to the treasurer.

Clerk to furnish abstract for the Comptroller.

SEC. 95. If any clerk shall fail to perform any of the duties required in the two preceding sections of this act, or shall falsely certify to the abstract of the sheriff's return, he shall be deemed guilty of a misdemeanor, and on conviction, shall be removed from office.

Forfeiture of clerk.

SEC. 96. If any person taxed in schedule B, of this act, refuses or fails to pay the taxes imposed, and leaves the county before the sheriff can collect the forfeiture, the sheriff, in his own name, may recover the tax and forfeiture out of the delinquent, in any superior court of the State; the tax and forfeiture when collected, shall be paid over by the sheriff, as originally required.

Penalty for refusing or neglecting to pay tax.

SEC. 97. The following subjects shall be taxed the amounts specified, and the taxes collected and accounted for thus:

Special subjects of taxation.

(1.) Every corporation that might become incorporated by letters patent, under the provisions of chapter 26, Revised Code, entitled "corporations," but shall fail to do so, and apply to the General Assembly and obtain a special act of incorporation, or shall obtain an act to amend their charter,

Corporations.

whether it had been secured by letters patent under said law, or by a special act, twenty-five dollars for each act, to incorporate or to amend, which tax shall be paid to the treasurer of the State.

Corporations not to organize till tax is paid. (2.) No corporation shall organize under such special act of incorporation obtained as set forth in the preceding section, or derive any benefit under such act to amend their charter, until it shall first have obtained a certified copy of such act from the secretary of State, and the secretary shall, in no case, furnish such copy until the company applying shall have delivered to him the treasurer's receipt for the tax assessed in the preceding section, which receipt the secretary shall file in his office.

Marriage license, mortgages, &c. (3.) Every marriage license, one dollar; every mortgage, deed, marriage contract, and deed in trust, made to secure debts or liabilities, one dollar; and every other deed conveying title to real estate, where the consideration is three hundred dollars or upwards, fifty cents, payable to the clerk of the county court. No clerk shall grant such license, or admit to probate such instrument, until the tax shall have been paid, and the receipt shall be endorsed on such license or instrument, and be registered with the same.

Brokers. (4.) Every broker, not a resident of the State, shall pay to the cashier of the bank from which he draws any exchange or specie, one per cent on all such sums drawn, to be accounted for to the State treasury, by the said cashier on oath.

Bank taxes. (5.) The president or cashier of the banks herein named, on or before the 1st day of October in each year, shall pay into the public treasury the following tax upon each share of stock owned by corporations or individuals, to-wit: The Bank of Washington, twenty-five cents; the Merchant's Bank of New Berne, twenty-five cents; the Bank of Wadesboro' twelve and a half cents; the Bank of Fayetteville, twelve and a half cents; the Commercial Bank of Wilmington, twenty-five cents; the Farmers' Bank of North Carolina, twenty-five cents; the Bank of North Carolina, ninety cents; the Bank of Lexington, forty-five cents; the Miners' and Planters' Bank, forty-five cents; the Bank of Commerce, forty-five cents; the Bank of Clarendon, forty-five cents; the Bank of Cape Fear, ninety cents; the Bank

of Wilmington, ninety cents; the Bank of Charlotte, twelve
and a half cents; the Bank of Yanceyville, twenty-five
cents; the Bank of Thomasville, forty-five cents; the Bank
of Roxboro, forty-five cents, and any other which may be
chartered by this or any future General Assembly, ninety
cents on the share of one hundred dollars, and in that pro-
portion for shares of a less value, and in case the said officers of any bank shall neglect or fail to pay the tax herein
required, said bank shall pay double the amount of said tax,
and the same shall be sued for and recovered by the Attorney General in the name of the State, in the superior court
of the county of Wake.

Sec. 98. Every clerk shall keep a record of the taxes re-   Clerks to
ceived by him, and to the county court next preceding the   keep a record.
first of July of each year on the first day of the term, shall
return a statement setting forth the date of each receipt,
the person from whom received, the subject on which received, the amount received from each person, and the aggregate amount received up to that date, and not previously accounted for; and to this statement the clerk shall at-
tach an affidavit that such statement is correct, and that no
receipt by himself or a deputy of his, has been omitted to
the best of his knowledge, which affidavit shall be sworn to
and subscribed in the presence of the chairman of the court,
who shall attest the same; and the county court clerk shall
record such statement and affidavit in a book kept for that
purpose in his office, and keep a copy of the same posted in
some conspicuous place in the court house, from the time at
which the return shall be made, until the first day of January next ensuing. And on or before the second day of the
term, the clerk shall pay the sheriff the amount of the taxes
received, as set forth in said return, less three per cent.
commission for receiving and accounting for said taxes.

Sec. 99. If any clerk shall fail to perform any duties re-   Penalty upon
quired in the preceding section, he shall be deemed guilty   clerks.
of a misdemeanor, and on conviction shall be removed from
office. And if any clerk shall fail to pay over to the sheriff
the amount of taxes in his hands on the day specified, the
sheriff shall inform the county solicitor of the default, and
the county solicitor shall bring suit on his bond, and shall

recover, in addition to the taxes withheld or not accounted
for, one hundred dollars, and the whole recovery shall be
paid into the treasury by the sheriff.

Settlement with Comptroller. SEC. 100. The sheriff, and all receivers of public monies,
shall yearly settle their accounts with the comptroller, be-
tween the last day of July and the first day of October,
(unless where the settlement of such person may be specially directed to be made in another manner, or at another
time) so that it may be known, what sum each one ought
to pay into the treasury ; and the comptroller shall forthwith report to the public treasurer the amount due from
each accountant, setting forth therein, if a sheriff's account,
the nett amount due from the sheriff to each fund, and
therefor the treasurer shall raise an account against such
person, and debit him accordingly.

To return the sources of taxation. SEC. 101. The sheriff in making his settlement, as aforesaid, shall designate in a list by him rendered at the time,
the different sources from which were raised the taxes accounted for by him, and the particular amount of tax received from each source ; and the comptroller shall give to
each sheriff a certified copy of such list, which the sheriff
shall deposit with the clerk of the county court of his county, for public inspection. In such settlement the sheriff
shall be charged with the amount of public tax as the same
appears by the tax list transmitted to the comptroller ; also,
with all double taxes, and taxes on unlisted property by
him received, and with all other tax which he may have
collected, or for which he is chargeable.

Credits to sheriffs. SEC. 102. He shall be credited (1) with the amount of
State tax on land bid off by the State, with the cost attendant on the sale, and procuring of the title, and with commissions on the whole, including the county revenue, on
producing the certificate of the secretary of State, as provided in section —— of this act. (2.) With all insolvent
taxables allowed by the courts as hereinafter provided ; and
when the sheriff shall be required to settle before such taxables are allowed, he shall be credited with them in the
next year's settlement, or the sheriff may, at any time thereafter, on producing certificates of such taxables allowed,
and procure an order from the comptroller on the treasurer

for the amount thereof. And in like manner, the sheriff shall have credit for any over payment made in former settlement, by reason of any error in the clerk's abstract of taxables.

Sec. 103. No insolvent taxables shall be credited to the sheriff in his settlement with the comptroller, but such as shall be allowed by the county court, a list whereof containing the names and amounts, and subscribed by the sheriff, he shall return to the court at some time preceding said settlement, and the same shall be allowed only on making oath that he could not find in the county, property of the tax payer, wherewith to discharge his taxes, or such part thereof as is returned unpaid, and that the persons contained in the list were insolvent at, and during the time when, by law,'he ought to have endeavored to collect their taxes. Such list shall be recorded on the minutes of the court, and a copy thereof, within ten days after its return, shall be set by the clerk in some public part of the court-house ; *Provided,* That when the sheriff may be desirous of obtaining his allowance for insolvent poll tax, that instead of swearing to his list, as the law now directs, the same may be submitted to the county court, a majority of the justices being present, who shall consider and examine said sheriff's list, and make him such allowances as they may think just and proper.

Sec. 104. If any sheriff shall return to court as insolvent, the name of a person who is not listed, or has paid his taxes for the year, or shall, by himself or his deputy, collect from any person his tax for the year, for which he has been returned an insolvent, without accounting for the same ; or if any clerk shall fail to record or set up the returns as required in the preceding section, the person so offending shall forfeit and pay to the State one hundred dollars, and the county solicitor shall prosecute a suit for the same.

Sec. 105. Every sheriff or other person allowed by law to collect and account in his stead, on settling his accounts with the comptroller, shall take the following oath, administered by the comptroller, and subscribe the same in the presence of the comptroller, by whom it shall be attested, and the comptroller shall make no settlement with the sher-

[marginal notes:] Insolvents.

Return of insolvents, &c.

Oath of sheriff and other collectors.

iff, or any one in his stead, unless he shall have sworn to and subscribed the oath as hereby required :- I, A. B., sheriff of the county of ——, do, on this, the —— day of ——, one thousand eight hundred and ——, make oath, that the list now given by me, is, to the best of my knowledge and belief, complete, perfect and entire, and doth contain the full amount of all monies by me or for me received, or which ought to have been received on account of the public taxes for the year one thousand eight hundred and —— on listed and unlisted property, and all double taxes, and all taxes received from clerks of courts, and from insolvents not heretofore accounted for, and all taxes received, or which ought to have been received from any other sources whatsoever. And I do further make oath, that if I, or any person for me, shall hereafter collect any unpaid tax now due, and not rendered in said list, I will render a true account thereof within one year after collecting the same.

False returns. SEC. 106. If the comptroller at any time shall have just cause to suspect that any sheriff, or other person accounting in his stead, may have made a false return, or sworn falsely in any matter relative to collecting or accounting for any tax, he shall thereof inform the officer prosecuting in the superior court of the county wherein the offence was committed, who shall take such steps as public justice may demand.

Sheriff's compensation. SEC. 107. The sheriff for his services in collecting and paying the public taxes into the treasury, shall receive a compensation of two per cent. on the nett amount received by him from the clerk for taxes imposed by schedule C, of this act, and four per cent. on the amount of taxes collected from every other source, to be deducted in the settlement of his account with the comptroller ; for collecting and paying county taxes (for whatever purpose laid) the sheriff shall receive the same per centum compensation as above allowed on public taxes.

SEC. 108. And for his settlement with the treasurer, he shall be paid by the treasurer three dollars for each day he may be necessarily engaged therein, and ten dollars for every thirty miles of twice the estimated distance from his home to the seat of government, by the most usual common highway.

SEC. 109. In every case of failure by the sheriff or other accounting officer to settle his accounts within due time, or to take the oath required on his settlement, the comptroller shall forthwith report to the treasurer the account of such sheriff or officer, deducting therefrom nothing for commissions or insolvents, but adding thereto one thousand dollars for the amount of taxes supposed not to appear in the list transmitted by the clerk, and if the whole amount be not paid the treasurer, on motion of the attorney general in the superior court of Wake county, at the first court after the default shall have occurred, shall recover judgment against such defaulting officer and his sureties for the amount reported against him, without other notice than is given by the delinquency of the officer. *Penalty for failure to settle.*

SEC. 110. The clerk of the county court at the same time when he transmits to the comptroller the tax list, shall transmit to him also a copy, certified under the seal of the court, of the official bond of the sheriff, conditioned for the collection, payment and settlement of the public taxes, upon the pain of his default of forfeiting to the State one thousand dollars, which the treasurer shall, and is hereby specially charged to collect in like manner, and at such time as is provided in the preceding section. *Official bond of sheriffs.*

SEC. 111. The register of every county yearly, on or before the first day of September, shall transmit to the comptroller a certified copy of the bond of the clerk of the county court, as the same is registered, upon pain of forfeiting, for his default to the State, one thousand dollars; which the treasurer is hereby specially charged to collect in like manner and time, as is provided in section 109 of this act. *Duty of Register.*

SEC. 112. In all suits directed by any law to be instituted on motion of the attorney general, at the instance of the treasurer or comptroller against any sheriff or clerk, and his sureties, a copy of the bond of such officer, certified as aforesaid, and sent to the comptroller, and by the comptroller certified, together with the default under his hand, shall be deemed sufficient evidence of the execution of such bond, and the default of the officer, to allow the judgment to be entered. *Suits against sheriffs, &c.*

SEC. 113. And in case of the default by the register to duly certify and transmit the bond of the clerk in proper time, the comptroller shall forthwith proceed to procure such certified copy, and also a copy of the bond of the register certified by the keeper thereof, and shall proceed in the manner hereinbefore provided, against them and their sureties at the first superior court in Wake county, after copies shall have been procured. *Default of Register.*

Default of clerks, sheriffs, &c.

SEC. 114. In every case of default, by any clerk, sheriff or taker of the tax list, or assessor of the value of property in the discharge of any of the duties of this act, imposed on any of them where no penalty is provided, the defaulting officer shall forfeit and pay to the State for each default, one hundred dollars. And all the penalties by this act imposed on such officers for the sole use of the State, may, when there is no special mode provided for recovering the same, be recovered in the name of the State, at the instance of the treasurer or on motion of the attorney general, or any of the solicitors of the State.

Comptroller's certificate to be evidence.

SEC. 115. The certificate of the treasurer or comptroller of any matter of default in any of said officers occurring at the office of the comptroller or treasurer, and copies of any papers in said offices duly certified by the proper keeper thereof, shall be admitted as evidence in any suit or prosecution whatever against them or others, and about any other matter whatsoever.

Treasurer may obtain judgment.

SEC. 116. The treasurer may, on motion, obtain judgment in any court of record against any person indebted to the State in the same manner and under the same rules and regulations which are prescribed in case of delinquent sheriffs; and the court shall award execution, though the amount of the claim be within the jurisdiction of a justice of the peace.

Penalty for perjury.

SEC. 117. If any person shall, wilfully and corruptly, commit perjury in any oath required to be taken or administered by any section of this act, such person shall be deemed guilty of a misdemeanor, and on conviction shall be subject to the same pains and penalties as are imposed in section 29, chapter 34, entitled "Crimes and Punishments," in the Revised Code, on persons guilty of perjury.

Repeal of former statutes

SEC. 118. All laws imposing taxes, the subjects of which are revived in this act as imposing taxes upon subjects other than those revived in this act, are hereby repealed; *Provided*, that this repeal shall not be construed to extend to the provisions of any law, so far as relates to the taxes listed, or which ought to have been listed, or which may be due for the year 1862, or for any year previous thereto.

Repeal.

SEC. 119. All other laws of this State, coming in conflict with the provisions of this act, are hereby repealed; *Provided*, that nothing herein contained shall be construed as repealing existing laws, authorizing the appointment of tax collectors in certain counties, and all tax collectors so appointed, shall be subject to all the provisions of this act as fully as sheriffs are declared to be.

SEC. 120. In all the counties of this State, where the first term of the county court, next after the first of January, is

already past by, or where, if held between the first of Jan- Order where County Courts
uary and the first Monday of March, it shall pass by without have passed, &c.
appointing assessors and tax listers, as hereinbefore provided ;
or wherever in any county the first term of the county
court shall be after the first Monday of March, the chairman of each of the said county courts, or if there be no
chairman, then the clerk shall direct a notice to the justices
of the said courts, to meet in their respective court houses,
to make the appointments aforesaid, and the clerk shall
record on the minute docket of his court the proceedings of
the said justices in special session ; *Provided*, that this section shall continue in force during the year 1863, and after
that, proceedings shall be had according to the previous sections of this act.

Sec. 121. As early as practicable after the ratification of
this act, the comptroller shall have published three thousand copies of the same for the sheriffs, clerks, assessors,
tax listers, and members of assembly, and shall distribute
the same among the different counties of the State, by such
mode as he and the public treasurer may adopt.

SEC. 122. This act shall be in force from and after its
ratification.

Read three times and ratified in General Assembly, this
11th day of February, A. D. 1863.

R. S. DONNELL, S. H. C.
GILES MEBANE, S. S.

STATE OF NORTH-CAROLINA,
OFFICE OF SECRETARY OF STATE.

I, JOHN P. H. Russ, Secretary of State in and for the
State of North Carolina, do hereby certify that the foregoing is a true copy of the original on file in this office. Given
under my hand this 20th day of February, 1863.

JNO. P. H. RUSS,
Secretary of State.

AN ACT SUPPLEMENTAL TO AN ACT PASSED AT THE PRESENT SESSION OF THE GENERAL ASSEMBLY ENTITLED REVENUE.

SECTION 1. *Be it enacted by the General Assembly of the State of North Carolina, and it is hereby enacted by the authority of the same,* That in all the counties of this State

Special courts may be called to levy taxes, &c. where the regular terms of the county court shall come after the listing of taxes in the year one thousand eight hundred and sixty-three, between the sending in of the lists to the clerk and the first Monday of June inclusive, the taxes for county purposes may be levied; and when the courts shall come after that day, a special court shall be called by the clerk or chairman, to be held prior to the first day of June, 1863, to make the said levy, and the proceedings of the same shall be recorded by the clerk on his minutes.

Court House. SEC. 2. Wherever, in the said act entitled "Revenue," the term court-house shall be applied, it shall be held to include all such places as may be used by authority of law for the holding of courts or the doing of the county business.

SEC. 3. *Be it further enacted,* That this bill shall be printed with the Revenue Bill.

SEC. 4. *Be it further enacted,* That this act shall be in force from and after its ratification.

Read three times and ratified in General Assembly this 11th day of February, A. D. 1863.

R. S. DONNELL, S. H. C.
GILES MEBANE, S. S.

STATE OF NORTH-CAROLINA, }
OFFICE OF SECRETARY OF STATE, }

I, JNO. P. H. RUSS, Secretary of State in and for the State of North Carolina, do hereby certify that the foregoing is a true copy of the original on file in this office. Given under my hand this 20th day of February, 1863.

JNO. P. H. RUSS,
SECRETARY OF STATE.